# S. S. I. M. –ple
(Stock Selection Investment Methodology)

# HANDBOOK

A BRIEF INVESTMENT REFERENCE GUIDE
*A three step process*

Amar Mehta

## STOCK SELECTION & INVESTMENT METHODOLOGY

Over the years, as I have conducted research, analysis, and portfolio management and progressed in my career -- from a lowly analyst to a portfolio manager, and eventually the Head of an Asset Management division – I had the privilege of working with some brilliant people. I also had the opportunity to train a few. This is a guide that I have developed and shared with my colleagues and other professionals, whom I have trained. Hopefully, it can be of some service to you in your investing endeavors.

It's a SSIM-ple approach and one that I think is worth incorporating, at least partly if not entirely, into any investor's toolbox.

Now, as with any recipe, the outcome is only as good as the ingredients, preparation, and attention to detail. I am only providing the framework for what I know works consistently in all markets, sectors, and cycles. Take from it what you need.

Lastly, as a computer engineer by education, I cannot help but share a quote from a notable textbook from my artificial intelligence class:

*"I think that it's extraordinarily important that we in computer science keep fun in computing. When it started out, it was an awful lot of fun. Of course, the paying customers got shafted every now and then, and after a while we began to take their complaints seriously. We began to feel as if we really were responsible for the successful, error-free perfect use of these machines. I don't think we are. I think we're responsible for stretching them, setting them off in new directions, and keeping fun in the house. I hope the field of computer science never loses its fun. Above all, I hope we don't become missionaries. Don't feel as if you're the Bible salesman. The world has too many of those already. Don't feel as if the key to successful*

*computing is only in your hands. What's in your hands, I think and hope, is intelligence: the ability to see the machine as more than when you were first led up to it, that you can make it more."*
Alan J. Perlis[1]
Structure and Interpretation Computer Programs, by Abelson and Sussman

This quote obviously can apply to many industries, including investment management.

I present this methodology in a similar vein.

---

[1] Alan Jay Perlis (April 1, 1922 – February 7, 1990) was an American computer scientist known for his pioneering work in programming languages and the first recipient of the Turing Award. Source: Wikipedia

# S.S.I.M.

## Stock Selection & Investment Methodology

### By Amar Mehta

The following pages provide the basic outline of the methodology.

After that, I provide brief commentary.

I have also shared this with a number of executives from large institutional money management firms – in a couple of cases they directly asked if they could use this internally.

**Step 1:**

**The Basics of Potential Investment (PI)**

I. **Understand the Industry Dynamics, Size, Growth of Potential Investment**
    i. What is size of market, growth potential, historic growth?
    ii. What are the industry drivers?
    iii. Factors that need monitoring or understanding present/potential factors affecting industry dynamics
    iv. Competition and what changes can affect that
        1. New entrants vs. change in technology or regulation
    v. How is PI positioned within industry

II. **Business Model of Potential Investment**
    i. Earnings drivers and Expense drivers / Margin analysis
    ii. Build Model using historic data, industry drivers, management strategy, and project "LIKELY" outcome (see chart)
    iii. Includes detailed understanding of financials
    iv. Meeting with management
        1. Understand Management Dynamics
    v. Perform sensitivity analysis for other possibilities

III. **Determine Target Valuation**
    i. Comparables on various industry specific metrics
    ii. DCF (if applicable), DDM, etc..
    iii. Sum-of-the-parts

**Step 2:**

**Determining Timing and Size of Potential Investment**

I. **Price Movement**

   i. Analyzing Discrete Historic Price Movements (accounting for market based activity vs. company specific)

II. **Catalysts**

   i. Understanding and Recognizing Historical and Potential Catalysts
   ii. Using Regression Analysis or other Historical Applied Methodologies to Determine future potential "LIKELY" outcomes based on catalysts

III. **Technical Analysis Overlay**

   i. Using Technical Analysis to add further support or credence to outcomes
   ii. Head/shoulders, Double-top/bottom, Breakout-volume based, Oscillators, Bollinger Bands, etc.

**Step 3:**

**Understanding Market Environment (SENTIMENT)**

I. **Mosaic Approach**

   i. Taking into account Step 1 & 2, one should generally be able to infer overall market sentiment regarding industry and stock

II. **Who is the Axe?**

   i. Sell-side and buy-side on the stock
   ii. Understanding what factors are relevant to the Axe
      1. note if step 1 & 2 are done to perfection then look in mirror!

III. **Shareholders**

   i. Know the main shareholders their strategy and reasons for investment
   ii. Sell your idea to new and existing shareholders if different and/or unique

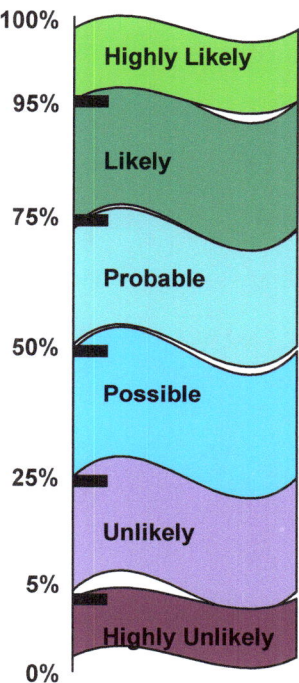

Step 1 should help identify long/short bias and Steps 2 & 3 should help determine timing and size of investment. Each investment is unique and denotes which Steps need more focus. Note, Step 1 is the starting point for any good investor. For hedge fund managers whose monthly P&L is of greater importance, Steps 2 & 3 are that much more. This is a general outline, but provides a good framework for stock selection and investment.

**Step 1:**

**The Basics of Potential Investment (PI)**

This is a very important part of the methodology from the perspective of understanding what you are looking at, investing in, and what is a fair price.

**Part one**, of Step 1, is simply what is the industry, and how does this company fit in that ecosystem?

**Part two**, is more detailed in that we want to know what are the levers that drive the company's profitability and growth. Building an earnings model is KEY. I cannot stress this enough. Guidance from the company can help with operating metrics. For larger, more economic sensitive companies, there are generally some revenue correlations that can be assessed. As no one has the ability to (legally) predict the results, there is generally a range of scenarios, i.e. best case, worse case, likely. Depending on your conviction level you can assign a probability, either based on historical patterns and/or your subjective assessment. This will help quantify your conviction level.

**Part three**, is valuation. There are many ways to value a company. I can write a whole book on that subject alone, and many have. Different companies require different approaches. You need to find the one that best suits your company.

So, now you know have an idea of the company, its drivers, and its potential valuation.

Note, meeting with management and key competitors is vital in forming a more current and realistic earnings and valuation model. This will help separate your analysis from the herd, because you will hear it from the proverbial 'horse's mouth' and you also have a basis of comparison versus other analysts and reports.

**Step 2:**

**Determining Timing & Size of PI**

**Part one** is about understanding what has moved the stock price in the past. You must differentiate between market related moves and those that are company specific. What times and periods does company specific information have greater influence over the stock price?

**Part two** is knowing the catalysts. What drives the stock price? Is it their monthly release of operational data? Is it their quarterly earnings? What about their annual shareholder's meeting? Is it their scheduled meetings, announcements, or events? Does its competitor or supply chain company's data release affect your company's stock price? This will allow you to know when you need to be more focused on either increasing or lowering your position.

Regression analysis is a very helpful tool with regards to finding out what correlations there are and of what significance.

**Part three** you can look at technical analysis as a guidepost on whether or not what you are seeing fundamentally, have seen historically, and what you expect to see in the future is being represented technically. I am not a technician. However, there are a number of good technical analysts and books that can guide you through this process.

Knowing what will move the stock price towards your valuation target and having a road map with regards to potential catalysts, you can set up your portfolio to maximize returns. You can increase or decrease your allocation accordingly. This takes time to master.

**Step 3:**

**Understanding Market Environment (SENTIMENT)**

**Part one** is about seeing the forest from the trees. In Steps one and Steps two, you focused on the company and all the intricacies of the business model and its impact on price movement. Now, sit back, get a cup of tea (or coffee, or other non-alcoholic beverage) and put down on paper a brief summary justifying your conclusions. This might allow you to see things a bit differently and also give birth to new ideas or questions. What are some external, exogenous forces that may come into play that might impact your conclusion?

**Part two** is knowing where the expectations are being set. We have all seen this where even if a company has bad results in the absolute sense, the stock outperforms. The market is a relative game. You need to know what the expectations are and who is involved in helping set those expectations. If your analysis shows, with the right amount of conviction, that the results are likely to be different than there MIGHT be an opportunity to exploit.

**Part three** is knowing why others, namely the largest shareholders, are invested in the company. Is it management? This can be a good thing, but you should also be aware of their motivation when they speak. If the larger funds are pensions funds, mutual funds, or hedge funds, you should find out what their approach is, so you have an idea why they are in the stock. The reason is simple; the largest shareholders have a significant influence over the stock price, not only from an entry/exit standpoint, but also from a perception standpoint.

This outline I have provided is broad and general. There are many nuances that I have glossed over. However, it is a good starting framework and requires proper dedication.

Questions / Comments / Suggestions ?

Email: SSIMBOOK@GMAIL.COM

Following pages left blank for your notes...

www.ingramcontent.com/pod-product-compliance
Lightning Source LLC
Chambersburg PA
CBHW041624180526
45159CB00002BC/999